Collins Englis|

C000185421

Amazing Thinkers
and Humanitarians

Level 4
CEF B2

Text by
Katerina Mestheneou

Series edited by
Fiona MacKenzie

Collins

HarperCollins Publishers
77–85 Fulham Palace Road
Hammersmith London W6 8JB

10 9 8 7 6 5 4 3 2 1

Original text
© The Amazing People Club Ltd

Adapted text
© HarperCollins Publishers Ltd 2014

ISBN: 978-0-00-754499-8

Collins® is a registered trademark of
HarperCollins Publishers Limited

www.collinselt.com

A catalogue record for this book is available
from the British Library

Printed in the UK by Martins the Printers

All rights reserved. No part of this book
may be reproduced, stored in a retrieval
system, or transmitted in any form or
by any means, electronic, mechanical,
photocopying, recording or otherwise,
without the prior permission in writing
of the Publisher. This book is sold subject
to the conditions that it shall not, by way
of trade or otherwise, be lent, re-sold,
hired out or otherwise circulated without
the Publisher's prior consent in any form
of binding or cover other than that in
which it is published and without a similar
condition including this condition being
imposed on the subsequent purchaser.

HarperCollins does not warrant that
www.collinselt.com or any other website
mentioned in this title will be provided
uninterrupted, that any website will be
error free, that defects will be corrected, or
that the website or the server that makes it
available are free of viruses or bugs. For full
terms and conditions please refer to the site
terms provided on the website.

These readers are based on original texts
(BioViews®) published by The Amazing
People Club group.® BioViews® and The
Amazing People Club® are registered
trademarks and represent the views of the
author.

BioViews® are scripted virtual interview
based on research about a person's life and
times. As in any story, the words are only
an interpretation of what the individuals
mentioned in the BioViews® could have
said. Although the interpretations are
based on available research, they do not
purport to represent the actual views of
the people mentioned. The interpretations
are made in good faith, recognizing that
other interpretations could also be made.
The author and publisher disclaim any
responsibility from any action that readers
take regarding the BioViews® for educational
or other purposes. Any use of the BioViews®
materials is the sole responsibility of the
reader and should be supported by their own
independent research.

Cover image © ryby/Shutterstock

MIX
**Paper from
responsible sources**

FSC
www.fsc.org **FSC™ C007454**

FSC™ is a non-profit international organisation established to promote the
responsible management of the world's forests. Products carrying the FSC
label are independently certified to assure consumers that they come from
forests that are managed to meet the social, economic and ecological needs
of present and future generations, and other controlled sources.

Find out more about HarperCollins and the environment at
www.harpercollins.co.uk/green

◆ CONTENTS ◆

Collins Amazing People Readers are collections of short stories. Each book presents the life story of five or six people whose lives and achievements have made a difference to our world today. The stories are carefully graded to ensure that you, the reader, will both enjoy and benefit from your reading experience.

You can choose to enjoy the book from start to finish or to dip in to your favourite story straight away. Each story is entirely independent.

After every story a short timeline brings together the most important events in each person's life into one short report. The timeline is a useful tool for revision purposes.

Words which are above the required reading level are underlined the first time they appear in each story. All underlined words are defined in the glossary at the back of the book. Levels 1 and 2 take their definitions from the *Collins COBUILD Essential English Dictionary* and levels 3 and 4 from the *Collins COBUILD Advanced English Dictionary*.

To support both teachers and learners, additional materials are available online at www.collinselt.com/readers.

The Amazing People Club®

Collins Amazing People Readers are adaptations of original texts published by The Amazing People Club. The Amazing People Club is an educational publishing house. It was founded in 2006 by educational psychologist and management leader Dr Charles Margerison and publishes books, eBooks, audio books, iBooks and video content which bring readers 'face to face' with many of the world's most inspiring and influential characters from the fields of art, science, music, politics, medicine and business.

◆ THE GRADING SCHEME ◆

The Collins COBUILD Grading Scheme has been created using the most up-to-date language usage information available today. Each level is guided by a brand new comprehensive grammar and vocabulary framework, ensuring that the series will perfectly match readers' abilities.

		CEF band	Pages	Word count	Headwords
Level 1	elementary	A2	64	5,000–8,000	approx. 700
Level 2	pre-intermediate	A2–B1	80	8,000–11,000	approx. 900
Level 3	intermediate	B1	96	11,000–15,000	approx. 1,100
Level 4	upper intermediate	B2	112	15,000–18,000	approx. 1,700

For more information on the Collins COBUILD Grading Scheme, including a full list of the grammar structures found at each level, go to www.collinselt.com/readers/gradingscheme.

Also available online: Make sure that you are reading at the right level by checking your level on our website (www.collinselt.com/readers/levelcheck).

Confucius

◆ ◆ ◆

551 BCE–479 BCE

the great Chinese philosopher

He who learns but does not think is lost. He who thinks but does not learn is in great danger. Real knowledge is understanding that we actually know very little.

◆ ◆ ◆

I was born a very long time ago – the story of my life was not written down until a long time after my death, so many of the facts are uncertain. But here I will tell you what was believed about my life and the events that shaped my thinking. I was born in China in the summer of 551 BCE – nobody can agree on the exact date and naturally I was too young to remember it myself. I was born in the village of Zou, in the state of Lu, near present-day Qufu in Shandong Province. My father was from an <u>aristocratic</u> family of warriors – brave, experienced fighters – and he died when I was three years old. This is not surprising when you know that he was about forty years older than my mother. Despite his family background, my father left us little money – the family had lost their fortune some time before – and we were often hungry. In Shandong Province, the winters were extremely cold, and just staying alive was difficult at times. I managed to bring in some money by working as a shepherd – looking after sheep – and I also took care of a local farmer's cows, so we did not <u>starve</u>.

My mother did her best to educate me and she taught me many fine lessons about life. The hours I spent with the animals gave me the chance to think about life and what made it good. I asked myself about how we should live, what was fair and unfair and how people should live together. As I grew older and became a teenager, these questions became all the more important to me. When I was 19 years old, I met a girl called Qi Guan. Within a short time we had got married and by the time I was 20, we had started our family. After the birth of our son, King Li, we went on to have two more children but our marriage was not a happy one. When I was 23, my mother died which affected me deeply for the next three years.

After my mother's death, I started studying philosophy. Already, one of my 'life' questions had been answered – as a family we learnt to understand each other's emotional needs. However, as I had a wife and children and all the extra costs that came with a family, I had to make sure that our practical needs were <u>met</u> as well as our emotional ones. I needed to make some more money. Because I could read and write, and many people at that time could not, I found a job as a clerk – keeping records and doing the accounts – for the Duke of Lu, the ruler of the state.

Lu was a powerful man who spent every day making decisions about other people's lives. Some people thought he was fair while others felt that he was against them. According to the way each person had been treated, I saw happiness, sadness and anger in their faces. Understanding how much we are affected by the things that people say and do, I developed my Golden Rule – you should not do to others what you would not like them to do to you. Each day at work, watching how people made decisions, I formed my views. The solutions to the questions that I asked myself were tried and tested each day and people came to respect me. I enjoyed working hard and I tried to be reliable, both of which were noted, and I was promoted.

✦ ◆ ✦

I lived during what became known as the Spring and Autumn Period in Chinese history. The country consisted of many small states that were constantly fighting for power. Chinese society was going through many changes as traditional values were challenged. There was tension and stress all around me and I wanted to find a way in which we could live in harmony – a state of peaceful cooperation. I had very clear views on how people should behave towards each other. Everyone had a specific place in society and according to where they fitted in, they had different roles to play and had different duties that they were responsible for.

Taking this a step further, I believed that there were five different types of relationships in the world. The first was between ruler and subject – the person living under the authority of the ruler. The second was that between father and son. The third was between elder brother and younger brother. The fourth was between husband and wife, and the last was between friend and friend. Apart from the last type, all the others involved one person having authority over another. The person who was not in the <u>superior</u> position of authority had to <u>obey</u> and respect the person who was, and the one with all the power had a duty to be responsible for and kind to the other. In my language, I called this duty to be a loving person *ren*.

◆ ◆ ◆

In 518 BCE, I left my job and spent my time reading and teaching. My aim was to encourage and <u>motivate</u> my students, not just to tell them what was right and wrong. It didn't matter to me who my students were or what social class they belonged to, I just loved teaching. This was unusual because at that time, education was something only the rich had access to. My approach seemed to be popular because it wasn't long before I had a large number of followers – people who supported me and believed in what I was saying. I decided to travel to the <u>imperial</u> capital of China, Lo-yang, so that I could learn about the customs and traditions of the <u>empire</u>. Then, in 517 BCE, when I had come back, the state of Lu was involved in war and I left again, along with the Duke of Lu, and went to a neighbouring state called Qi. Here I learnt about music. The next period of my life was spent with my followers and I was also a teacher.

At the age of 51 in 500 BCE, I became the Justice Minister of the state. This was a job that required balance between the law and politics and I saw myself not as an inventor of the

China at the time of Confucius

law but a messenger of it. In each case I listened to, all the facts had to be collected, and then <u>interpreted</u> and <u>applied</u>. I believed that having a moral viewpoint, rather than just following the law, was vital. People would ask me if we needed laws. My answer was that if people always behaved well to each other, then that would be enough, and no, it was not necessary to have laws. But people can be <u>greedy</u> and unfair, wanting more than their fair share, in which case, society cannot function without laws.

Another one of my beliefs was that we should appreciate our ancestors because without them we would not be here. I thought that it was vital to show respect for our living <u>elders</u> and family members, because without them, we would be alone. For me, the basis of a strong community was helping others, in the hope that they would help you in return. Life is a series of choices, choices which can benefit some people and disadvantage others. But it can be difficult to put the needs of others before the things we ourselves want. I believed that one of the keys to happiness was to understand other people and their needs. Another key was to be virtuous and by that, I mean behaving in an honest and moral way.

However, it is much easier to be virtuous in thought than it is in practice. For example, nobody wants to find themselves in the position where they may lose other people's respect. This may happen if you make a stupid mistake. To avoid looking stupid, we sometimes try to hide the mistake we made and in the process we make more mistakes. I always thought that it was better to be honest and admit making the first mistake. In this way, not only do we avoid making the original situation worse, but also we can learn and improve, and make fewer mistakes in the future. But to do this, you have to get to know yourself. Knowing yourself is the first step in understanding other people. Without this first step, you will not be able to live with other people in a calm and pleasant way.

As well as asking me about the necessity of laws, people around me were curious about religion. Did we need to have religion in our lives, they asked me. My answer was that I did not find religion logical. All religions have ideas of what is good and bad, and often the religious rules as to what is allowed and what is not allowed are not flexible enough. Society changes but these rules stay the same. Another aspect of religion that I had difficulty with was the existence of a god. Was it possible that there was one god only, and that this god had all the answers? I doubted it very much. What I didn't doubt was the need for some kind of belief system, but I didn't know what form it should take.

In contrast, I truly believed in democracy. At any one time, there can only be one ruler but it should be the people who decide who is going to govern. Cruel and unfair rulers can then be removed from power. I saw leadership as being a gift, not an absolute right, and I believed that the person given the honour of ruling should be a virtuous person at all times. If they do not behave in a correct, <u>ethical</u> way, then people will rebel and choose a new leader. I knew that this system would work well in a small place where everyone knew each other, but I was not sure if it could be applied to somewhere much larger. How could a ruler communicate his beliefs and rules in an area where great distances had to be covered? If his word was not widely known, how could it

A Chinese temple

be supported? If a leader was not supported, he could not be respected, and without respect, his future was at risk.

Virtue, for me, was the all-important characteristic for a leader. If people were ruled by laws and were punished when they broke them, they would try to avoid the punishment but would not change their behaviour. However, if a ruler was a virtuous person and ruled by example, that is, by always behaving in a moral and ethical way, then people would change their 'bad' behaviour and would start to be virtuous, too, without needing to be punished.

I stayed in my position as Minister of Justice in the state of Qi for four years and in that time, I was promoted to Prime Minister, but due to serious political disagreements, in 495 BCE I decided to leave both my job and the state of Qi. I travelled, going from one region to another, always in the company of my followers. I talked to people wherever I went, hoping that some of my <u>principles</u> would be adopted by them. I was especially hopeful that rulers would lead their people based on a system of virtue, but I did not see many examples of this. In 483 BCE, I returned to the state of Lu and continued my teaching. In 479 BCE, when I was 72, I died. My followers treated me as if I had been their father, and as was the custom at the time, <u>mourned</u> me for three years. After my death, my followers started to write down some of my theories and they produced a publication now known as the *Analects*. My beliefs could now be taught by others to later generations of students. In this way, the <u>philosophical</u> school of thought, Confucianism, was born.

The Life of Confucius

551 BCE	Confucius was born in the village of Zou in the Chinese state of Lu, near present-day Qufu, Shandong Province.
548 BCE	When Confucius was three, his father died. He was raised by his mother, in poverty.
532 BCE	Aged 19, he married Qi Guan and they had a son and two daughters. He worked as a shepherd, cowherd, clerk and book keeper. Due to his ability to read and write, he secured a job with the Duke of Lu, as a clerk.
528 BCE	His mother died and he spent the next three years in mourning. During that time, he studied philosophy. He wanted to create harmony among people in his home country of China which was in conflict and fighting many wars.
519 BCE	Confucius began teaching ancient customs. His teachings were based upon moral and ethical principles for day-to-day living. He believed that there were five different relationships in the world.

518 BCE   He travelled to the imperial capital, Lo-yang, and studied the traditions of the empire.

517 BCE   When there was war in the state of Lu, the Duke of Lu and Confucius escaped to the neighbouring state of Qi. Confucius learned the art of music.

500 BCE   At the age of 51, he was appointed as the Minister of Justice of the state of Lu. He was promoted to Prime Minister.

495 BCE   Confucius left the state of Lu and his position in the government. He spent the following years travelling from one region to another hoping to put his principles into practice.

483 BCE   He returned to the state of Lu and refused any offer of a Government position.

479 BCE   Confucius died aged 72, in the state of Lu.

Socrates

♦ ♦ ♦

*c.*470 BCE–399 BCE

the great Greek philosopher

My greatest belief, and one that guided me my whole life, was a simple one. If you have a problem and want to find the solution that is right for you, you have to make sure you ask the right questions.

♦ ◆ ♦

I was born in the city of Athens, Greece in 470 BCE. My father, Sophroniscus, was a stonemason – someone who cuts stone for building work – and <u>sculptor</u> and my mother, Phaenarete, was a <u>midwife</u>. As you can imagine, we were not wealthy and we lived a simple life. I had the most basic education and then when I had finished school, my father taught me his trade. I also learned a great deal by watching him as he worked. Being a practical man, my father let his hands, rather than his mouth, do the talking. I trained myself to pay attention to detail and I tried to be a good <u>apprentice</u>, working hard.

Even though I tried, I was not very interested in becoming a stonemason. My real passion was listening to the stories the <u>elders</u> in our village told. Each day, I would hear these wise old men sharing their views with whoever would listen. They talked about what they knew, and their opinions differed depending on how they saw life. They would discuss problems of the present, such as how our way of life could be improved. They would look at examples from the past to help them reach conclusions. Ideas for the future were also considered, for example, whether new laws should be introduced to improve society and if so, which ones. Apart from practical issues, they also discussed more abstract topics, such as whether truth and certainty actually existed. Each would try to convince the others that their view was the correct one. Those who were respected for their attitude and contributions – for they were not all judged equally – usually had the most success.

To me, these debates were at the centre of reality. Unlike the lifeless stone and wood that I worked with every day, people were warm and alive and were capable of thought. I believed that it was our duty to share and compare what was in our minds in order to improve and develop as human beings. This and only this would lead to happiness and a contented, rich life. I had seen that wealthy people were not necessarily happier than the rest of us.

I had noticed that there are times in our lives when difficult decisions have to be made and we don't know which direction to take to get the best result. Let me explain what I mean. From an early age I had seen people – my mother is a good example – worry about areas of their lives that

A Greek chariot

they thought were problematic. As with all families, we had plenty of disagreements. My mother found it difficult to keep the peace and be fair at the same time. At times I am sure that I was responsible for making her upset and angry but often she didn't ask me why I was behaving badly. Instead, she would decide for herself what was troubling me and would act accordingly. She wasn't always right and I discovered how important it was to share thoughts and ideas.

♦ ◆ ♦

In 431 BCE, the Peloponnesian War between Athens and Sparta began. I was a soldier at the time, doing my military service. In the heat of battle there was little time for debate and sharing one's thoughts – differences were settled by fighting – but having a set of <u>principles</u> did help to guide me. I tried to be brave and fearless. People later told me that I was. I was lucky enough to be able to save the life of an Athenian general called Alcibiades, who was respected and well-liked in Athens.

Greek society in the 4th century BCE was divided up into cities, each functioning as a state with its own government and rules. It was normal for them all to be in conflict with each other, but there was an alternative way of dealing with such conflicts – a great competition that we called the Olympic Games. The original Olympics were held in honour of Zeus, who, according to Greek <u>mythology</u>, was one of the twelve gods who lived in the temple of the gods at Mount Olympus. Zeus was the father and king of the gods. In the town of Olympia a huge, impressive statue of him was built and Greeks from all over the country came to see it. It was here that the Games were first held.

All the Greek city states sent representatives to compete in the games. Everyone taking part had to swear an <u>oath</u> to the king of the gods, and had to be able to speak Greek. It was important not only for the athletes to compete in sporting competitions, but also to participate in the many theatre, poetry, sculpture, dance and singing events that were held. The Games were the perfect occasion for everyone to celebrate their culture, their religion and their artistic talents.

In the beginning, the sporting competitions were open to both men and women, with the women taking part in a series of races called the Heraean Games, <u>dedicated</u> to the goddess Hera. Later on, however, women were excluded from competing and then were not even allowed to enter the stadium. Eventually this rule was relaxed and women were permitted to compete in equestrian events, that is, those involving horses. A Spartan princess called Cynisca, driving a four-horse <u>chariot</u>, was the first woman to become an Olympic winner.

Statue of Zeus in Olympia

In contrast, the first male Olympic champion was a man called Coroebus, a cook who won the first running event which covered the distance of 192 metres. For the men, there was a variety of events, all designed to test mental and physical strength as well as <u>endurance</u>. It was a rule that athletes had to train for at least ten months before the Games. Winners did not get medals. Instead, they were given a crown made from leaves, called a laurel wreath. They were also given a branch from an olive tree. As well as becoming a valued sporting event, the ancient Olympic Games became a great social occasion, too. People from the city states who were not athletes would meet to share ideas and do business and in this way the Games helped develop Greek culture and way of life.

But, of course, real life was not just about taking part in sporting and cultural events, nor was it about being polite to each other. Politics, too, had its place and where there was politics, there was also conflict, caused by various types of bad behaviour. People tried to dominate each other; they tried to cheat each other; and they were jealous, wanting what their neighbours had and they did not.

I had become interested in philosophy, and I was wondering about how social conditions could be improved, for example, how could we avoid injustice? I developed a method of investigation which people later called the Socratic Method. It consisted of my asking people, both rich and poor, questions based on political and <u>ethical</u> issues. The topics covered, among other things, courage, love and respect, and the way people saw themselves. I questioned anyone I found out and about in the city streets and I didn't care whether they were willing or not to talk to me. I must have developed a particular style because young people would copy the way I talked. From people's answers I intended to create what I saw as being 'truths'. I would have the evidence I needed to state that I had more than just a theory. I would then use my evidence to try and make a better world and better living conditions. But finding real evidence could be difficult because people didn't always want to answer my questions. When they did answer, they were often not truthful. I believed that those who were <u>reluctant</u> to give answers were those who had something to hide. I soon discovered that it was the honest people who had no problem with telling the truth.

I also believed that for the better world I was looking for to exist, politics had to be conducted in a honest way. That came back to people again. The government worked best when it was ruled by individuals who had the greatest ability and knowledge, and <u>possessed</u> a complete understanding of themselves. The only way to achieve this understanding was to ask the right questions and answer them truthfully.

When I was 50, after I had spent many years on my work, I met a woman many years younger than me, called Xanthippe and in 419 BCE we became husband and wife. We had three children, all boys, and although I would like to say our family life was happy, it was not. Xanthippe always felt that I did not pay enough attention to her and the boys. I am afraid that she may have been right.

◆ ◆ ◆

In 404 BCE, after 25 years of conflict and fighting, Athens had been finally defeated in the last battle of the

Peloponnesian War. The city was now going through a period of <u>instability</u> and its people were feeling <u>insecure</u>. They did not wish to let go of their memories of successful battles, their ideas of wealth and their obsession with physical beauty. Good looks were seen as being incredibly important for anyone wanting to be successful in the world of politics. For a long time, beauty and the idea of goodness had been linked. If you were not handsome, people thought you could not be a good person either. My own appearance did not help me as I could not have been described as being good-looking by anyone, probably not even my own mother. Nor was I interested in money and what it could buy. This was probably a good thing as I was always rather poor. I did not try to look like a successful man by wearing good clothes or by trying to look clean and tidy. I tried to convince society that it was the mind that was of the greatest importance. Unfortunately many people felt threatened by what was, in their view, an attack on their way of life. I tried to use humour while I was challenging their conventional wisdom but I was not always very successful and I managed to upset both politicians and the military.

A military government called the Thirty Tyrants took control of the city and they ruled for about a year. During that time, I became even more unpopular with the authorities. On one occasion a man had been sentenced to death and I thought the way he had been judged was unfair. I objected, as I was not the kind of man who kept quiet about social injustice. Once again, speaking my mind led to some dangerous situations. However, my message must have had some influence because in 406 BCE I was invited to be a member of the Boule.

The Boule was a council made up of city residents. It dealt with matters such as property disagreements and access to the facilities in the city. For the council to be successful, it had to be fair and make decisions that people could accept, but there were often problems. Other members of society who were not part of the council wanted things to happen their way. They knew that money was a powerful tool and they used it to get what they wanted. Justice was replaced by <u>corruption</u>, something that I found unacceptable. I protested, with the result that I made more enemies.

I had not stopped using my method of asking questions to find solutions, but the questions that I asked those in power gave offence. The truth was often inconvenient, for if they answered truthfully, they would expose themselves as being dishonest or corrupt. Still, I did not give up and with every question I raised, the political temperature also rose. I have to admit that I quite enjoyed seeing these people arguing. At least they were talking about what was right and wrong. As it turned out, though, they were also talking about me and what was to be done with me.

During 399 BCE, a message arrived saying that I was going to be arrested. Friends advised me to escape but to me that was to admit defeat. I had always thought that running away from a problem was no answer. The right thing to do was to face my accusers, so that's what I did. There were many of them. A jury of 500 Athenian men were <u>gathered</u> to judge me. At that time, religion was a serious thing in Athens. There were many religious festivals that people, by law, had to take part in. The many temples and shrines – the places where people went to pray and <u>worship</u> – were cared for with public money. Showing religious disrespect was a serious crime. My accusers claimed that I did not believe in the Athenian gods, but worshipped gods of my own. They believed that my attitude was dangerous and that my views were corrupting young people, who were also behaving in a disrespectful way. Others accused me of <u>interfering</u> with progress. Few people openly said what really scared them but I knew what it was. I was the voice of the poor people, the majority of citizens who could not vote and could not be heard. What would happen if I was allowed to become their political champion? Would there be a revolution? Would we win? That was the real fear!

Realizing the danger of allowing me to be free, the majority of the powerful 500 had their way, and I was found guilty of being a revolutionary. I was imprisoned, but I was not a murderer or a thief. I was really guilty of two things, neither of which I considered to be a crime. One was searching for truth and the other was trying to <u>abolish</u> inequality from society. I was sentenced to death by poison, which I drank myself. The end of my life, however, was not the end of the search for justice and truth, and it certainly did not stop my ideas from taking on a life of their own. I like to think that my principles of <u>ethics</u> and morality had considerable influence on the development of scientific thought.

The Life of Socrates

*c*470 BCE   Socrates was born in Athens. He was
the son of Sophroniscus, an Athenian
stone-mason, and Phaenarete, a midwife.
Socrates learnt his father's trade at a young
age. His interests were in ideas and later
he focused on education and philosophy.

459 BCE   Socrates gained a basic education and
through his curiosity, he began to learn
about the customs and culture of Athens.

449 BCE   He was probably working in his father's
business at this time.

439 BCE   Socrates was developing his philosophy,
based on asking questions about social
life. These covered issues such as what is
justice and what is goodness.

435 BCE   About that time, Socrates developed the
view that the best way to a happy life is
to focus on self-development, rather than
chase after wealth. Building relationships
came before making money.

431 BCE   The Peloponnesian War began (Athens v. Sparta). Socrates participated in three military campaigns during the war, at Potidaea, Deliurn and Amphipolis, as a soldier. He saved the life of Alcibiades, a popular Athenian general. Socrates was known for his courage and fearlessness in battle.

425 BCE   Socrates continued to raise questions about social life and may have earned his living as a teacher.

418 BCE   Socrates fought in the Battle of Mantinea.

419 BCE   At the age of 50, Socrates married Xanthippe, who was much younger. They had three sons: Lamprocles, Sophroniscus and Menexenus.

412 BCE   Socrates had the opportunity to try out his theories and ideas, as a parent. He continued to make speeches and attract the interest of the poor people and the youth, as well as annoying some politicians and military people.

404 BCE   The Peloponnesian War ended. Athenians
           entered into a period of instability and
           doubt about their identity. Socrates was
           critical of leaders who had failed in the war.

406 BCE   Socrates was a member of the governing
           organization called the Boule.

407 BCE   He met Plato and shared his ideas. Plato
           wrote up his memory of the meetings,
           which served as a record, as there was no
           direct evidence of Socrates writing a book
           of his philosophy or psychology.

400 BCE   Socrates called himself a philosopher
           and social critic. Many people listened
           to his criticism of the politicians and
           military leaders. He was seen by some
           as a revolutionary, who encouraged the
           ambitions of the poor.

399 BCE   Socrates was sentenced to death for
           being a revolutionary. It was said that
           he worshipped new gods of his own
           and not the Greek gods and that he was
           encouraging young people to do the same.

Aristotle

• ◆ •

384–322 BCE

the first man to organize scientific knowledge

If you ask people to mention the names of three great philosophers, my name will come up along with those of Socrates and Plato. People also remember me because Alexander the Great was my most famous student.

◆ ◆ ◆

I was born in 384 BCE in Macedonia in the north of Greece in a town called Stagira, which was a busy port. Nowadays, many tourists want to see the place that is famous because it was my birthplace. There isn't much left of the old town, just ruins, but people enjoy seeing part of the wall that surrounded the town, some of the old houses in it and the market place – the Agora. This was the most important part of the town because it was here that people went to do business, talk politics and of course socialize.

I was lucky enough to have parents who taught me many things, but you could also say that I was rather unlucky, too, because they both died when I was just a boy. My father, whose name was Nicomachus, was a doctor but he wasn't an ordinary doctor. He was the personal physician to King Amyntas of Macedonia. It was my father who made me interested in learning about medicine. Naturally we didn't really know very much about how the human body worked, nor did we know exactly what caused people to become ill. When they were sick, we tried to cure their illnesses with herbs and prayers. What we did understand, however, was that keeping fit by taking regular exercise was extremely important. We saw that those who were fit got ill less often than those who never exercised at all.

Medicine wasn't the only subject I was interested in. By nature, I was a curious child and, from an early age, I listened with great interest to the family discussions that often took place at home. These debates – because they were more than just discussions – were about the political situation in our town. They focused on the activities of all the influential people who lived there. I don't know whether or not it was my father's wish for me to become a politician. Unfortunately, he died long before I knew myself what I wanted to do with my life.

When my father died, leaving me an orphan, my older sister Arimneste and her husband Proxenus took me in and looked after me. My father had been a wealthy man and there was plenty of money available for my education. In addition to my existing interest in politics and medicine, what I was really fascinated by was philosophy and science. Not only did I want to continue my studies in these subjects but I also wanted to study in the city that was the most important

Greece in the time of Aristotle

academic place on the planet. So in 366 BCE, at the age of eighteen, I packed up and moved to Athens.

◆ ◆ ◆

Athens was a completely new world for me. My first impression was of all these city people rushing noisily through the streets trying to make their fortune. They were so busy in their attempts to make money that very few of them actually had the time to discover new things and explore the world around them. This, however, was exactly what I intended to do with my time. Having come from an <u>aristocratic</u> family, I had enough money to follow my dream and to live comfortably.

In Athens, I joined Plato's Academy. Plato was a great thinker and teacher and I learnt a great deal from him. For the next twenty years, until his death, I worked at the Academy. It was the perfect chance to research and teach and I focused on the 'science of living' which included politics, physics, <u>logic</u>, biology and psychology. In one sense, original thought was easier in my time because there was so much that we didn't know. We could research a subject, and with the results, we could expand and develop what we already knew about it.

When Plato died in 347 BCE, many people believed that I would become the new director of the Academy, but I was not offered the position. Before his death, Plato had requested that it would be his nephew, not I, who would <u>inherit</u> the position. During our time together Plato and I had had many academic differences and it was <u>inevitable</u> that we would disagree sometimes. Perhaps his decision was based on these differences, perhaps not, but anyway, I decided instead to travel.

Travelling was hard work and took a long time on dangerous rough roads. I walked, or rode on horses or camels, whatever the weather. In the summer, it was hot and dusty; in the winter, I froze in the snow, ice and fierce winds. In autumn and spring, I got very wet when it rained. Of course, every season had its spectacular moments but there was no doubt that however rich you were, travelling was uncomfortable.

When I finally reached Assos in Asia Minor, I visited an ex-student of mine, Hermias, who had once been a slave. As well as gaining his freedom, he had managed, surprisingly, to become King of Atarneus. I stayed with Hermias's family for three years and met his niece, Pythias. We fell in love and got married. I was already a happy man, but one of the best days of my life was when little Pythias, our daughter, was born.

◆ ◆ ◆

In 343 BCE King Philip II, whose son would become Alexander the Great, invited me back to Macedonia to educate the thirteen-year-old boy, and there I became the head of the Royal Academy. I taught Alexander and a few of his friends philosophy, poetry, drama, science and politics. Alexander dreamed of being a hero on the battlefields and, when he was 16, he took part in his first battle. Two years after that, he helped his father to defeat armies from both Athens and Thebes. King Philip II was head of the Corinthian League and he managed to get all the Greek city states, with the exception of Sparta, to agree to belong to it. When Philip died in 336 BCE, Alexander became King of Macedonia, but being King did not give him the right to be the leader of the League. Athens was being ruled by Dimosthenis, whose aim was to control the League himself. Alexander sent his army south and persuaded the members of the League to accept him as their leader.

◆ ◆ ◆

In 334 BCE, while Alexander was fighting for control of Asia, I decided to return to the city with my family. I still wanted to teach and I was given permission to open my own school, at the edge of the city, which we called the Lyceum. I gathered together a group of research students who became known as the 'peripatetics'. Their name was based on the Greek for 'walking' because of their habit of wandering around the school while they were thinking and discussing different topics. I wanted education to be available for everyone and so many of our lectures were open to the public and were free of charge. It was in this school of mine that my type of thinking was given a name: 'Aristotelian logic', the key aspect of which was clarity of thought, and here I wrote, among many others, two of my better known books: *De Anima* and *Parva Naturalia*.

Academic life wasn't easy. We worked by the light of candles which was hard on the eyes, and it was often cold. It wasn't only at the Lyceum where conditions were difficult. Poverty and disease surrounded us and tragically, because we did not have enough knowledge of medicine to save her, my poor wife died in 335 BCE at a very young age. I was sure that we wouldn't have lost her if our level of education had been higher and we'd been able to carry out proper scientific research.

◆ ◆ ◆

Education, in my view, consisted of three parts and to be thorough and correct, had to include all three: the practical, the poetical and the <u>theoretical</u>. The practical covered politics and <u>ethics</u> in government and business, the poetical was concerned with the arts and <u>humanities</u>, while the theoretical was all about mathematics and <u>metaphysics</u>. The scientific method that I was in favour of provided a link between the three areas, but I was convinced that evidence, rather than just opinion, had to be the basis for assessment. The problem with evidence, however, was that it was proving hard to find for many of my theories.

Before I returned to Athens and set up the Lyceum, I had gone to the island of Lesbos for a while in the hope of finding such evidence. I wanted to study natural life in its natural form. In the sea, marine life provided new understanding and I was completely fascinated by botany – the study of plants. I knew that plants had secrets that could bring help to those who were ill. I had learnt that much from my father, but I was sure that there was still so much more to be discovered. In the field of agriculture, too, we had to find better ways of growing crops so that we could become more efficient at feeding ourselves.

In contrast, I believed that because the study of ethics is a personal subject, the best way to learn about it was through life experience. By 'life experience' I mean learning by thinking about the decisions we make and the things that we do. This means studying our thoughts as they are acted out. Politics, however, is a public matter. People in general use

Aristotle

politics to survive. It is all about using your skills to <u>negotiate</u> who gets what, when and how. Depending on how good you are at politics, the results will either be positive with peace and <u>prosperity</u> all around you, or negative, leading to a state of conflict and revolution.

Philosophy became a key area of my thought and teaching as I tried to find a way to integrate logic, feelings and evidence. Later, much of my approach was adopted and turned into what was called Scholasticism and some of my ideas were kept alive. In a world where time destroys almost everything, my life's work has survived. Not only has it survived, it is now better known than it was when I was alive, although it did disappear for a while. In about 1500 CE, after hundreds of years in a world where science was forgotten, my work suddenly came to life again as universities began to teach Greek. My work became visible and important once more. However, much of what I suggested then was guesswork. My claim that the earth was the centre of the universe took more than 2,000 years to be proved.

Theory is fine, but scientific evidence is hard to establish because it requires clear thinking and the strength not to give up. Theories are ideas that mark the way for change and development. To get evidence, experiments need to be made and we need to learn from our actions. We need more people to face the challenge of the unknown, people who will advance understanding, despite the ignorance of others.

Innovation takes time to succeed, and it seems to be a fact that having evidence by itself is not enough. It is also necessary to have a quick mind and make good judgments. You need to be able to publicize your ideas and have the confidence to tell the whole world about them and make people believe in you. Only in this way can people move forward.

In 323 BCE, Alexander the Great died and the Macedonian government lost power. In Athens there were considerable anti-Macedonian feelings and I felt that my life was in danger. I made the decision to leave the city and to go to the island of Euboea. A year later I died there of natural causes.

The Life of Aristotle

384 BCE   Aristotle was born in Stagira, Chalcidice, near Thessaloniki, Greece. The name Aristotle means 'the best purpose'.

366 BCE   He was sent to Plato's Academy in Athens to study.

347 BCE   Plato died and Aristotle left Athens for Assos, Asia Minor. There he met a former student, Hermias, and later married Hermias' niece, Pythias. They had one daughter, who they also named Pythias.

344 BCE   Aristotle lived on the island of Lesbos for some time where he carried out botanical research.

343 BCE   Philip II of Macedonia invited Aristotle to tutor his son, Alexander (the Great) and he was appointed as head of the Royal Academy there.

334 BCE   He returned to Athens and established his own school, called the Lyceum.

335–323 BCE   His wife Pythias died and he then became involved with Herpyllis, with whom he had a son that he named after his father, Nicomachus. During these years, he wrote many of his works including *De Anima* and *Parva Naturalia*.

323 BCE   Alexander the Great died and anti-Macedonian feelings increased in Athens. Fearing a death sentence, Aristotle escaped to the island of Euboea.

322 BCE   Aristotle died of natural causes, aged 61 or 62, on Euboea.

William Wilberforce

◆ ◆ ◆

1759–1833

the man who ended the British slave trade

Freedom, <u>slavery</u> and Christianity – these were the words that had the biggest impact on my life. They began to influence my thinking and action as soon as I became <u>mature</u> enough to understand their true meaning.

◆ ◆ ◆

I was born in 1759 in the town of Hull, in the north of England. My father was a rich merchant and we lived a comfortable life. My parents were religious people, Christians, who often mentioned the word slavery. Of course, as a child it didn't really mean much to me, nor did the concept of freedom. I only knew that my own freedom to play and join in games with other boys was limited by my poor eyesight and bad health. When I was nine years old, my father died. My mother's grief was deep and resulted in her not being able to look after me, so I was sent south to London to live with my aunt and uncle.

Religion to them was more than going to church and praying, and they worked to end poverty and slavery. After a while, when my mother had recovered from my father's death, I returned home. However, I had been influenced by my time with my relatives in London and their views on life stayed with me. I was lucky having had a privileged upbringing but I realized that most people did not share my luck. When I was seventeen, I went to St John's College, Cambridge University. I had inherited money from different relatives, so with money of my own I was financially independent. This meant that I could do what I wanted and enjoy student life to the full. I experienced a world of luxury that most people at the time could only dream about while all around me there was poverty and misery.

I lived in an academic world where there was a lot of talking and very little action. Talking about the real world and the difficulties most people were facing was not enough for me. I knew that with my wealth, education and contacts, I could make a difference. My friend, William Pitt, who later became Prime Minister, suggested that I enter Parliament. He knew a lot of influential people and introduced me to political life. I managed to get elected – using eight thousand pounds of my own money undoubtedly helped – and in 1780 I became a Member of Parliament for Kingston-upon-Hull while I was still a student.

I decided not to join a political party but to be an Independent. In that way, I could lead rather than follow – I didn't want the restrictions that belonging to a party would involve. I had money, and with money it was possible to have influence. It was also possible to have a very enjoyable social life. In the evenings, I went to various gentlemen's clubs. These were clubs where upper-class men would meet their friends, enjoy expensive dinners, and <u>gamble</u>. Some said that I was clever with words, a talent that certainly helped me when speaking in Parliament. So my life as a wealthy politician began. It was a pleasant type of existence and while on a tour of Europe in 1785, I continued enjoying the privileged kind of life that money could buy. But something had started to worry me.

I began to question why, when Britain was a relatively rich country, there were very poor people in every town and city. There were people who were living in the most desperate poverty. The upper classes, however, were not only living well, but were increasing their wealth, for example by renting out land and property to the poor. My interest in spiritual matters grew and I started asking myself what sort of a life I should be leading. To find answers, I read the Bible and I realized that there was a better way. I wanted to share my beliefs and make other people think in the same way. Naturally, this affected my politics but I was doubtful if this was a good thing. Would people take seriously a politician who was as deeply religious as I was? I asked William Pitt, who by this time was Prime Minister, for advice, and he encouraged me to continue and to act on what I believed in. One of these beliefs was that slavery was wrong.

The British slave trade began in the 16th century when Britain began to acquire territories to add to its Empire. <u>Colonists</u> started farming the land and they needed workers. In the beginning, they hired people but as the farms grew larger, they needed more people than were available. In the British territories in North America, American Indians weren't suitable because they easily caught diseases the Europeans had brought with them like pneumonia and tuberculosis and they usually died as a result. The Portuguese and Spanish were already using slaves from Africa in their own colonies and so the British decided to do the same.

Most of the British slave trade was centred in the West Indies – a group of islands in the Caribbean – which was part of the British Empire. The main crop on the plantations was sugar, which was sent to Britain and other places in the Empire. The money that came from the plantations was invested by the owners in other types of industry such as banking and insurance, and Britain's economy became partly dependent on the slave trade. Slaves were not only a valuable source of income for the slave traders, they were also the main reason the plantations were so profitable. The owners did not have to pay wages and by encouraging female slaves to have children, there were future generations of workers born into slavery.

It was clear that British business people were leaders in the slave trade, although Portugal, Spain, France and North America were also involved. Our supply of sugar, coffee, tobacco, cotton, silver and gold was completely dependent on using slaves in the great plantations. By the 1730s some of the plantation owners, many of whom lived in Britain, had become extremely wealthy. They had also become members of Parliament. This meant that they were able to influence the laws dealing with the colonies of the Empire. For two hundred years, laws were not passed that would affect the source of their wealth – in this case, the slave trade.

The North Americans had declared independence in 1776. The colonists, many of them slave owners, had defeated the British army, and the United States of America had elected their own politicians and were making their own laws. However, it was British businessmen in British ships who were still running the slave trade. They had developed a three-way system, which was known as the triangular trade. Guns, alcohol and other goods produced in Britain were shipped from there to Africa. Then local rulers exchanged the goods for people – human beings who had been captured and had become slaves. The ships took the slaves across the Atlantic Ocean where they were sold to plantation owners. The ships, once they had delivered their human cargo, would load up with products like sugar or tobacco and would then sail back to Britain.

One evening at dinner, in 1783, I met a man called James Ramsay, who had been a ship's doctor in the West Indies and later a Church of England priest. He told me what he had seen on the ships arriving from Africa and I was horrified. Slave traders would travel to Africa to find or hunt and capture healthy-looking men and women, who were taken to large ships. They were chained together and put below decks with hardly enough space for them to breathe, let alone move. Conditions on the ships were terrible and thousands died during the voyage. When the ships arrived at their destinations, the slaves had to face the humiliating experience of being sold to their new owners. Those who had survived the trip were usually in the most terrible physical condition – at best, they were exhausted, starving and thin. On arrival they were washed, the men were shaved and oil was put on their skins to make them look healthier. When the slaves had been made to look as good as possible, potential buyers would come and examine them as if they were animals, to choose which ones they wanted.

The slaves were then sold in one of two ways. Sometimes an auction was held. At an auction, buyers would offer an amount of money for a slave and the person offering the greatest amount would be the one to buy him or her. On other occasions, the slaves would be put together into one room. The doors would open and the buyers would all rush in and grab the slave or slaves they wanted. Either way, it was brutal. The slaves did not know what was going to happen to them or where they were going to be taken, and they did not understand English. In total, more than fifteen

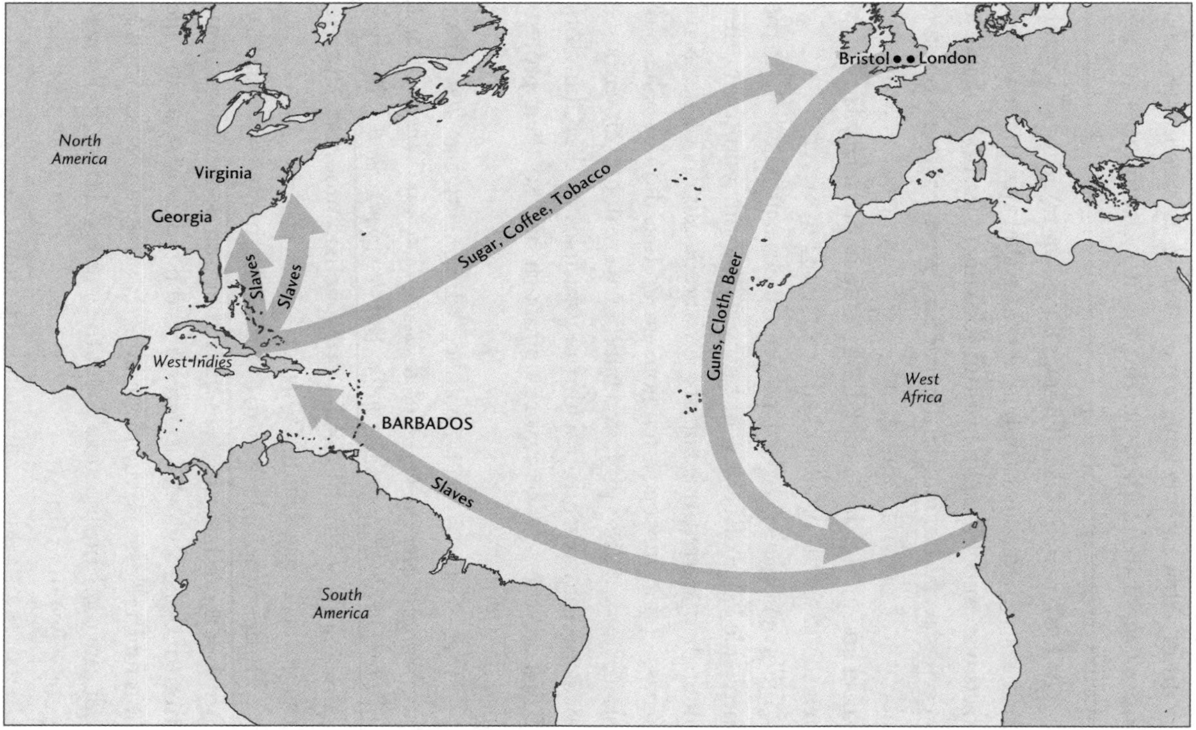
North America
Virginia
Georgia
Slaves
Slaves
Sugar, Coffee, Tobacco
Bristol
London
Guns, Cloth, Beer
West Indies
BARBADOS
Slaves
West Africa
South America

Trading in the time of William Wilberforce

million Africans became slaves and it was estimated that over two million died during the dreadful eight- to ten-week voyage from Africa.

In 1787, a man called Thomas Clarkson came to see me. He had researched and written an essay on the slave trade, and the facts were shocking. The British Parliament found itself able to accept slavery, but for me, the question was what could be done about it. Looking around me, at the sugar, cotton, tobacco, silver and gold that we took for granted in our everyday lives, I felt that everything I touched was <u>tainted</u> by slavery.

The people who had power in government had to be persuaded that slavery was wrong. Clarkson, with two other men, had started the Society for the Abolition of the Slave Trade. The Quakers, a religious group that did not believe in slavery or war, also protested but they were not taken seriously. Because they disagreed with the principles of the Church of England, the Quakers were unpopular and so their protests had little effect.

James Ramsay had published *An Inquiry into the Effects of Putting a Stop to the African Slave Trade* and *Treatment and Conversion of African Slaves in the British Sugar Colonies.* Because he was a Church of England priest he had more influence in the government than the Quakers.

Ordinary people had to be told the truth about slavery. Most of them had no idea where their sugar or tobacco came from and the few who did know had no idea how terrible life was for the slaves on the plantations. A campaign was started to educate the British people about the truth of slavery and slowly people began to listen.

From then onwards, I focused all my energy on trying to achieve my goal of making the slave trade illegal. Day after day and night after night, I tried to convince people. But it was a hard fight. All around me there were people – rich <u>influential</u> people – who benefited from slavery. In 1790, I was allowed to set up a committee to look at the slave trade and examine how it was operated. The following year I introduced the first bill to <u>abolish</u> slavery but the politicians voted against it. They said there were more important issues to be considered because of the threat presented by the French Revolution and the rise of Napoleon. They were also afraid of the new United States of America and questioned if it was right that we should <u>interfere</u> with their slave system. The politicians even went as far as to suggest that it was the Americans' job, not ours, to stop the practice of slavery. This did not stop me, however, and I continued to raise the question of slavery at every opportunity.

◆ ◆ ◆

I was so busy working and fighting for my beliefs that my personal life had suffered and I was alone. Romance was the last thing on my mind until I met the woman I would marry. In 1797 a friend introduced me to a young woman called Barbara Ann Spooner, whose smile filled me with joy. The day after I met her, I sent a note suggesting that we meet again. She agreed and we talked about my work. Within a few days, I had made up my mind and at a private dinner, I asked her if she would be my wife. To my delight she agreed and we starting making plans for our wedding. Our family and friends were not so enthusiastic as we had only known each other for eight days. Barbara may have been eighteen years younger than I was – which was not unusual at the time – but I knew I had found true love. In the next ten years we had six children and my life at home filled me with the strength to continue my battles at work.

My political campaign against slavery continued at full speed, gradually gaining support and on 22nd February 1807, the Slave Trade Act was passed, making the buying and selling of slaves illegal. The British Parliament had decided with 283 votes for, and only 16 against, the Act. The next year, the USA also made the slave trade illegal, but it did not succeed in actually stopping the trade of slaves, nor slavery itself. There was clearly a lot more to be done before the practice of slavery would end and the slaves would be given their freedom. In 1816, the names and personal details of all the slaves were written down in an official list, and I started looking at other important issues.

I wanted Parliament to pass laws to improve working conditions, especially for children and factory workers. What I did not agree with was giving workers the right to organize unions because I was worried that this would lead to revolution, as it had in France. I was also concerned about people's morals and I fully supported Bible studies for children at Sunday School as well as helping to establish the Church Missionary Society. But my focus remained on abolishing slavery.

In 1833, the Slave Abolition Act was passed, banning slavery in most colonies of the British Empire and giving the slaves their freedom.

Full credit should go to Thomas Clarkson and others for their efforts. By that time, I was nearly blind and very much poorer than when I had started my campaign. My death came within days of the passing of the Act but my <u>sacrifices</u> were minor compared to those of the slaves. While their 'Christian' owners had been seen praying in church, more than two million slaves had been killed, millions more had been beaten and countless were badly-treated and worked to death. With the 1833 Act, my life's work to ban slavery by the British had been achieved. But elsewhere the battle continued.

The Life of William Wilberforce

1759   William Wilberforce was born in Hull,
        Yorkshire, England.

1767   He began his schooling at Hull Grammar
        School.

1768   At the age of nine, William's father
        died. He was sent to live with his aunt
        and uncle at their homes in London
        and Wimbledon. William was sent to a
        boarding school in Putney and spent his
        holidays with relatives.

1771   William's mother and grandfather were
        concerned about his religious instruction,
        and therefore brought him back to Hull.

1776   He attended St John's College, in
        Cambridge. His grandfather died,
        followed by his uncle. Their deaths left
        William with his own money to spend as
        he pleased.

1780   While still a student, on September 11th,
        William was elected as a Member of
        Parliament for Kingston-upon-Hull.

1783   His friend, William Pitt, was elected
        Prime Minister.

1784   William was elected as a Member of
        Parliament for the county of Yorkshire
        in the general election. In October, he
        toured Europe with his mother, sister and
        Isaac Milner, the brother of his former
        headmaster.

1785   He returned to England to support Pitt's
        Parliamentary changes before continuing
        his travels to Italy and Switzerland.
        William read *The Rise and Progress of
        Religion in the Soul* which had a serious
        effect on him. He began to pray and read
        the Bible.

1786   William rented a house near Parliament,
        in Westminster. He used his position to
        promote changes in the law.

1787   Thomas Clarkson began calling on
        William and asked him to bring forward
        the case to the House of Commons for
        the Abolition of Slavery. The first meeting
        of the Society for Effecting the Abolition
        of the Slave Trade took place.

1789   On May 12th, William delivered his first
        speech in the House of Commons against
        the slave trade. He also introduced his first
        bill to abolish the slave trade.

1790 He gained approval for a Parliamentary Select Committee to consider the slave trade and examine the evidence.

1791 In April, the first Parliamentary Bill was introduced. It was defeated by 163 votes to 88. From then on, William introduced a motion of favour of abolition during every session of Parliament.

1793–1798 The war in France meant that although the subject of the slave trade continued to be debated in Parliament, serious consideration was never given to it.

1797 William met and married Barbara Spooner. They had six children over the next ten years.

1799 The Slave Trade Regulation Act was passed to reduce overcrowding on slave ships.

1804 William helped to start the British and Foreign Bible Society and the Church Missionary Society.

1806 The new Foreign Slave Trade Act was passed. It banned all British people from helping in any way or taking part in the slave trade to the French colonies. In effect, the Act stopped two-thirds of the British slave trade.

1807   On February 23rd, the British Parliament
        finally abolished the slave trade. Then
        on March 25th the Abolition of the Slave
        Trade Act was passed. It stopped the
        trading of slaves, but did not actually
        abolish slavery.

1822   William helped form the Anti-Slavery
        Society.

1823   He launched the campaign for slaves to be
        given their freedom.

1825   He retired from Parliament after 45 years
        of service.

1833   William died aged 73, in London,
        England. Just three days before his death,
        on July 26th, the Slavery Abolition Act
        was passed. Slavery was abolished in the
        whole of the British Empire and all the
        slaves within it were given their freedom.

Karl Marx

◆ ◆ ◆

1818–1883

the man who wrote
The Communist Manifesto and *Das Kapital*

I was not born into poverty but I hated the inequality between the very rich and the very poor. I spent my life, through my writing, fighting for equality. I believed that everybody, whatever their class and financial state, should have the same rights.

◆ ◆ ◆

I was born in 1818 in the city of Trier in Germany. My father was a lawyer and my mother had more than a full-time job looking after my father, myself and my eight brothers and sisters. We had a comfortable life and I didn't go to school until I was twelve because until that point I had been educated at home by private tutors. After attending the high school in Trier for five years, I went to the University of Bonn and studied law. Like many students suddenly thrown into an adult world, I found myself in a bit of trouble. I got into debt, had fights and once was even sent to prison. My father was not very pleased with my behaviour and insisted that I take my studies more seriously. At his suggestion – and as he was paying the bills, I didn't really have much choice – I moved to the University of Berlin, where I studied law and philosophy.

In Berlin I joined a group of students called the Young Hegelians, who were occupied with criticizing the political and religious authorities. The group was based on the teachings of the philosopher Hegel. I was not, in the beginning, that interested in his theories but I became an active member as my interest in politics grew. It was during this time that I met my future wife, Jenny von Westphalen. Jenny came from quite an upper-class family and there were many people who were interested in her apart from me. She was also four years older than I was. We got engaged, secretly, and did not get married until seven years later.

In 1841, I got my <u>Doctorate</u> in Philosophy but due to my political beliefs, which others saw as being extreme and unwelcome, I was not able to get a teaching position at the university. In fact, I was forced to leave altogether. The people in power were feeling increasingly threatened by the articles I was publishing which demanded a better life for the poor. I went to live in Cologne, where I started a <u>left-wing</u> political newspaper, then I moved to Paris for a short time, where Jenny and I got married. However, it didn't seem to matter where I went to live, because wherever I was, my views on life were unpopular.

After Cologne, the city of Brussels, in Belgium, seemed to be a good place to live and we stayed there for two years. I met my dear and life-long friend Friedrich Engels and also I became involved with people from the <u>Communist</u> League. The communists believed that the government should own a country's wealth – its industry, property and natural resources – and that it should be shared equally with everyone. They thought it was unfair that the upper classes and the <u>aristocracy</u>, who were a tiny minority of the population, should have so much while the working classes had almost nothing. The Communist League asked me to write down the <u>principles</u> of <u>communism</u> in a document that could be read and used by everyone, which I did. I explained in my writing that the working class is exploited by the upper-class capitalists whom I called the bourgeoisie. Capitalists get rich from the work done by the poor. The true value of something – goods or services – is the amount of work actually done. Any extra money that is made – profit – should belong to the people who did the work and not the capitalists. The only way that this situation can be changed is if the workers have the power to make rules. This can only be done if working classes take power away from the capitalists by using force and violence. No wealth should belong to individuals and all governments should be <u>abolished</u>. I ended with the following: 'Working men of all countries, unite!' My involvement in the League drew attention to my political views and I made yet more enemies by speaking out for change and equality. I was accused of trying to cause a revolution, but I answered that if a revolution happened, it would be the poverty of the people, not me, that was responsible. The poor were in the majority, but they had no votes and therefore no power to change the situation.

By 1849, many European countries were in the middle of bitter revolutions and it was then that Engels and I, now back in Cologne, published *The Communist Manifesto*, which was based on the written work I had done for the Communist League. This was seen as a huge challenge to the civilized life enjoyed by the upper classes, and the continuous threats that were being made to my life made it necessary for me to leave Cologne, too. I had not shot or injured anyone, but I was seen as an enemy, so I decided we should move to London. There I could write and spread my message through my publications. Perhaps the British would be more open to hearing what I had to say.

◆ ◆ ◆

Living conditions in Berlin, Paris and Brussels had been bad but the poverty and misery in London were far worse than anything I had ever seen. The streets were full of people who had no choice other than to steal food or even pick out <u>rotting</u> food from the rubbish to survive. Many had no homes and were forced to live on the streets, which were <u>filthy</u> and full of rats. Then there was the <u>workhouse</u>. In 1834 the first workhouses were opened. They were supposed to be places where people who had absolutely nothing could go and live. The government was afraid that 'lazy' people would take advantage and so conditions inside were made incredibly <u>brutal</u> and <u>humiliating</u>. They did provide food and shelter for those who would have died otherwise, but they were widely hated, so much so that many preferred to take their chances out in the streets than face the shame and <u>stigma</u> of the workhouse.

There had been much whispering of the word revolution and a group called the Chartists had long been planning a series of political attacks. The Chartists were an organization that wanted the government to be elected in a fairer way. They wanted every man over the age of twenty-one to have the right to vote. At the time, only men who had property that could be rented for at least ten pounds a year could vote. This meant that six out of every seven men did not have the right to vote. The Chartists were also campaigning for a more acceptable system of <u>representation</u> in the government. Large cities, where mainly poor people with no property lived, often did not have even one member of parliament representing them. Unfortunately, the Chartists were neither well-organized nor successful. I agreed with their principles and set to work in the British Library – where it was only possible to get access if you could prove you were a serious researcher – to write the plan that would get rid of capitalism. This would be a plan that would remove the great class divides between the rich and the poor.

My ideas were ahead of their time as the people in London had not yet heard about communism. In the north of England, however, factory and mine workers started to join together to form unions to try and negotiate with the government over working conditions. New innovations like electricity and gas were comforts for those who already had comfortable lives. The living conditions of the poor, who would not have either electricity or gas for a long time, were not getting better. In fact, life became worse as more and more people were attracted to the large cities. The major cities, already too full, were becoming unbearably overcrowded as people like myself arrived from Europe. In 1845-1846 a terrible famine happened in Ireland when that year's potato crop failed. The potato was one of the basic foods in Ireland and without it, people starved. The Irish who could, travelled to other countries. Many moved to the USA but many others came to England.

By 1849, 20 per cent of the population of London were now Irish and like my family, they were all immigrants – people who had come from another country in search of a better life. We lived at 28 Dean Street, and paid twenty-two pounds a year in rent for two basic rooms in very bad condition. It was very cramped as we were a large family. My wife gave birth to seven babies but only three of them lived to adulthood. This horrible situation was far from unusual and I was sure the terrible conditions – the <u>filth</u> and poverty – played a major role in the high death rate among children. My family's accommodation and living standards were far better than some, even though I was not able to earn a living. Nobody would employ me and if it had not been for the generous help of my friend, Engels, I do not think any members of my family would have survived at all.

The Dukes of Bedford, Norfolk and Westminster in their <u>country estates</u> were earning huge rents from the poor, who had to live in filthy, disgusting conditions. We all lived in the same country but it was as if we were in two different worlds: ours, the working class, and the other that belonged to the upper class. I could not accept that a person who was unlucky enough to have been born into a poor family was forced to live a life of misery. Across the English Channel, many countries were in a state of anxious confusion, with people demonstrating in the streets to get better conditions.

I was sure that this would happen in Britain, too. After all, it was the place where the Industrial Revolution had begun, I spent my days researching and writing. 'A <u>spectre</u> is haunting Europe,' I wrote. 'The spectre of Communism.' Looking around the miserable streets of London, I waited. Surely the working class would rise up and take action. But despite my best efforts to develop protest through my writing, there was no revolution.

Some capitalists had produced useful innovations – in addition to the gas and electricity we already had, the invention of the telephone improved communications. But despite this, the working people continued to be exploited in industry and agriculture, in the factories and fields. My proposal was to have a revolution by democratic means – let all men have the right to vote and elect the government of their choice and then if that was not successful, we would need to fight. 'From each according to his abilities, to each according to their needs.' That was the message I was trying to communicate in *Das Kapital* – the most famous of all my books. I wanted to look in more depth at what I had outlined in *The Communist Manifesto*. I tried to explain how capitalism had developed and what its future might be. I focused on economic theory and described more fully the relationship between workers and capitalists, showing how workers are exploited and giving specific examples from the past. My aim was to demonstrate that capitalism is unstable and why it should be abolished.

I believed there was a need for a 'science of society'. I saw that the class struggle was inevitable – the struggle between capitalism and communism or more simply, between the 'haves' and the 'have nots'. It would be an economic civil war that would change politics forever. In 1871, after the Paris Commune rebellion, where the people of Paris fought against the government, I wrote a pamphlet – a short book – called *The Civil War in France*, which became famous. I hoped that the struggle for equality would occur peacefully, but feared that it would not, especially not in my lifetime. In 1883, I died at the age of sixty-four, two years after the death of my wife, Jenny, and I was buried in Highgate Cemetery in north London.

The Life of Karl Marx

1818   Karl Heinrich Marx was born in Trier, in
        the Prussian Rhineland.

1819   The family moved to a ten-room property
        near the Porta Nigra, in Trier.

1830   Karl attended Trier High School after his
        private education ended.

1835   He studied law at the University of Bonn.
        The following year, Karl studied at the
        University of Berlin, where he continued
        to study law.

1837   Karl joined the Young Hegelians. He
        wrote a novel, *Scorpion and Felix* and
        a drama, *Oulanem*, but they were not
        published.

1841   Karl earned his Doctorate in Philosophy
        with his thesis *The Difference Between the
        Democritean and Epicurean Philosophy of
        Nature*.

1842   Karl lived as a refugee in Cologne,
        where he was a journalist for a left-
        wing newspaper called *Rhenish*. He later
        became the Editor-in-Chief.

1843   Karl married Jenny von Westphalen. They moved to Paris, where Karl studied political economy, the French socialists and the history of France.

1844   He met German socialist Friedrich Engels. *On the Jewish Question* and *The Economic and Philosophical Manuscripts* were published. The following year, he wrote *Theses on Feuerbach*, which was not published until after his death.

1845   Karl, Jenny and Friedrich moved to Brussels, Belgium. Karl and Friedrich published a criticism of the philosophical ideas of Bruno Bauer called *The Holy Family*. They visited London and met the leaders of the Chartists. With Friedrich, Karl wrote *The German Ideology*, which was published after his death.

1847   He wrote *The Poverty of Philosophy*.

1848   Karl and Jenny moved back to Cologne. He started the publication of the left-wing political paper, *New Rhenish Newspaper*. Karl and Friedrich published *The Communist Manifesto*. Europe was in the middle of violent revolutions.

1849   Unable to return to Germany or Belgium, Karl and Jenny moved to London, where he became involved in the German Workers' Educational Society.

1851   Karl wrote about the French Revolution of 1848, *The Eighteenth Brumaire of Louis Napoleon.*

1852   He wrote for the *New York Daily Tribune.*

1859   Karl published *Contribution to the Critique of Political Economy.*

1864   He became involved in the International Workingmen's Association and was elected to the General Council.

1867   The first volume of *Capital: Critique of Political Economy (Das Kapital)* was published.

1871   When the citizens of Paris rebelled against the government during the Paris Commune, Karl wrote one of his most famous pamphlets, *The Civil War in France.*

1881   His wife, Jenny, died.

1883   Karl died aged 64, in London, England.

Mahatma Gandhi

◆ ◆ ◆

1869–1948

the man who helped free India from British rule

All my life, all I ever wanted was for India to be an independent, united country. I wanted a peaceful end to 350 years of British rule. The British did leave but to my deepest regret, they left behind an India that was divided in two.

◆ ◆ ◆

I was born in Porbandar, a city on the west coast of India, where most people lived in poverty and <u>hardship</u>. We were lucky – my father was the chief minister of the city – so we had a decent standard of living. My mother was a true follower of Jainism – an Indian religion that believed, among other things, in complete self-control. This meant that although we were not poor, our lifestyle was a simple one. India was under the rule of the British Raj and many white men from the British Isles were sent to our country. They forced their law on us, but could not change our customs and beliefs.

Map of India before independence

People who believed in Jainism thought that differences between people should be solved with respect, <u>mutual tolerance</u> and understanding – not violence. I followed these <u>principles</u> faithfully my entire life.

I was married at the age of thirteen to a girl a year older than me who was called Kasturba. As was the custom, it was an arranged marriage with neither of us having any say in the matter. Over the years we had four sons, although our first child, born two years into our marriage, died just a few days after birth. Medical facilities were limited and basic and many babies and children died as a result.

I was fortunate enough to have a good education and I decided that I wanted to study law. I had heard a great deal about all the fine cities in Britain and the place I wanted to go was London, which, I had heard, was the greatest of them all. So, having gained a place at University College London, I left India. It was a complete <u>culture shock</u> to arrive in such a big city after living my whole life in Porbandar.

I was used to the heat of India, and the cold and never-ending damp of England was not a pleasant experience for me. I no longer kicked up dust on the roads of my hometown – in London you were more likely to be covered in mud than dust. Before, I had been just one of many. Now I was one of the few – an Indian man amongst the British. I was a long way from home and each day was a challenge. I spent many lonely days studying my law books.

Law to me was not just about what was legally right or wrong. I also wanted it to help people behave in a way that was socially acceptable and this meant looking at the principles behind the law. My early life in Porbandar influenced me greatly, as the Jainist principles I had brought with me guided me both in my studies and my social life. One of the battles everyone has to face is how to beat their own inner enemies, such as anger, <u>intolerance</u> and <u>immorality</u>. I believed that self-control was important and that taking responsibility for your own actions was essential. It was no use blaming someone else for your own bad behaviour or lack of <u>will-power</u>. Where I came from, these beliefs guided poor and rich alike but in London I found many different views.

It was not Jainism that was being debated but <u>capitalism</u> and <u>communism,</u> or democracy and <u>theocracy</u> and I found it fascinating to be exposed to so many new ideas. However, no matter what I heard, I held strongly to my beliefs and managed to resist all the temptations facing a young man in the city. In 1891, I graduated from university and was called to the Bar. I thought it was a strange expression, as if one was going to be served drinks but in reality, it meant that I had become a qualified barrister and could now represent people in the law courts.

♦ ♦ ♦

Two days after my graduation, on 12th June 1891, I set sail for India.

On arriving, instead of the joy I had been expecting at coming home, I was told my mother had died. Days of sadness were followed by hard times financially as I tried to care for my family. I set up a law practice in Mumbai but the lack of clients meant that I soon had to close it down. I decided to apply for a job as a school teacher but I was unlucky there, too, and my application was rejected.

In 1893, I accepted a one-year contract in the British <u>colony</u> of Natal in South Africa. It was a relief to have some paid work but <u>frustration</u> took its place as I experienced countless acts of discrimination. This is one example. One day I was travelling, quite legally, in the first-class carriage of a train, when I was told by a guard to go and sit in third class. When I refused to move, I was actually thrown off the train. My Jainist beliefs of tolerance for all people told me that action against prejudice was required. Realizing that the law was not enough to protect one's rights, I knew I had to do something myself.

• ◆ •

I decided to stay and campaign for civil rights for minority groups. The Natal Indian Congress was formed in 1894, providing the Indian community with a voice. I persuaded my family to join me in South Africa, but life there was not easy for us. I had seen poverty, injustice and suffering and my life-long aim was to bring about peace and <u>prosperity</u> all over the world. However, in South Africa it seemed a very long way away – for example, Indian marriages had been declared illegal. In 1908, I was arrested for leading <u>resistance</u> and spent two months in prison, which strengthened my determination to stand up for my beliefs. On the streets, prejudice against Indians remained. In 1913, I led 2,500 Indians in a protest and once again, I was arrested and put in prison.

In Europe the First World War had begun, with more violence and destruction than had ever been seen before. I was worried that such a conflict could happen in India. I wanted to help our nation develop in a peaceful way, which I called *Ahimsa,* but I didn't know what role I could play. South Africa was burning with racial conflict. We had children born in a country where Indians, an Asian minority, were always seen as immigrants. However, the Indian population was caught in the middle of a larger battle – the <u>tribal</u> groups fighting against the British and Dutch settlers. I wondered if I should be using my talents in my own country. After twenty-one years in South Africa, it was time to return to India. Aged 45, I took my family home.

◆ ◆ ◆

In India, we had the same issues of prejudice. Indians were subservient to the British and we were a divided nation under the Raj. We were also divided between Hindus, Muslims and other religions. My family and followers needed support and so I set up a farm, a place for them to go, called Sabarmati Ashram. I believed that Indians, not the British, should rule India, and my political campaign for independence began when I spoke at the Indian National Congress.

The turning point in my campaign happened when I visited a place called Champaran. Here my goal was to help poor farm workers working for British landlords. The British ordered me to leave, but I refused and told the workers to hold non-violent protests. I was arrested. Hundreds of thousands of people marched in mass protests and eventually, the law was changed, giving the farm workers more control. The 'satyagraha' non-violent approach had worked. News of the success spread through cities, towns and villages but the prejudice and violence did not stop. In 1919 in Amritsar, the Jallianwala Bagh massacre happened. 379 people were murdered and over 1,000 wounded, and I realized that self-government for India was essential.

By 1920, I was the president of the All India Home Rule League and our cry was 'Independence from the British Empire'. In 1921, the 'swadeshi policy' was introduced where we decided not to buy foreign goods, particularly cloth from Britain. Other protests were organized to raise political awareness but it was a long, slow and difficult process. Those in power were reluctant to admit defeat. Month after month, I travelled across India, encouraging people to protest. I was arrested and put in prison for two years for trying to make people <u>disobey</u> the government. No prison is pleasant but the conditions there were truly terrible. Despite this, they could not break my spirit and on my release, I became president of the Indian National Congress (the INC).

Support for our cause was growing and on 30th January 1930, I published the *Declaration of Independence of India*. I had not forgotten the bitter war that took place when the Americans made their own declaration of independence from Britain all those years before. I decided on non-violent action. On 12th March, I led a 385 kilometre march to the Gujarat coast in the west of the country. Here I committed an 'act of defiance' against the British, who had a <u>monopoly</u> of the salt production. I made salt from sea water. I was arrested for this 'crime' and immediately non-violent protest broke out across India, and thousands of Indians were imprisoned. News of this had spread across the world and the leader of the British in India, Lord Irwin, wanted *satyagraha* to end. I was released from prison and I promised to give up the *satyagraha* salt campaign on three conditions. The first was the release of those who had been imprisoned, the second was to allow Indians to make their own salt. The third was for the INC to be invited to the 1931 Round Table talks in London, where the future of India was to be discussed. Irwin agreed and on 5th March 1931 we signed the Gandhi-Irwin agreement.

I felt that the people of Britain needed to know more about our cause. While I was in England in 1931 attending the Round Table talks, I was invited by the Davies family, who owned several mills, to meet the mill workers in the north of England. The mills were the factories that made

cloth and many mill workers had lost their jobs when India stopped buying British cloth. The Davies family wanted me to see the hardship that the now unemployed workers were experiencing. I understood their difficulties and I tried to be sympathetic, but I wanted to make them understand how much worse living conditions were for the Indians. I hope I made an impression on them.

In 1932 I started another major protest against British rule. This time it was on behalf of India's disadvantaged lowest <u>caste</u>, the Dalits, better known as the 'untouchables'. I preferred to call them Harijans – 'God's Children'. The British rulers were planning a new political system that would increase discrimination against the Dalits, and would damage Hindu society. To gain attention, I refused to eat. To no one's surprise, I was again thrown into prison. Although I was furious, I kept to my principle of non-violence and I still refused to eat. After six days of fasting, it was agreed that the new system would not be introduced, and it seemed that our non-violent protest was again having an effect.

◆ ◆ ◆

There was, however, still much to protest about and I spoke at many meetings. The British officials objected and they arrested me again. Had they learnt nothing from the loss of their American colonies? How could such well-educated men act in such stupid ways? More long days were wasted in prison. As a lawyer, I knew the law but what good did it do me? On my release, I was 63 years old and it was time to travel. Over the next four years, I toured rural communities. The poverty was depressing, but the spirits of the people <u>uplifted</u> me and gave me new energy. However, far away, there was more conflict as the Second World War had begun.

As India was a British colony it became involved in the war, with many fine men going into battle. My principles of non-violence were tested to the full. Could one be a <u>pacifist</u> when mass murder was being committed? If it had been Jains instead of Jews being <u>gassed</u>, could I have stood by? The reality of Nazism and the death camps made me think about pacifism.

The major aim of the Indian National Congress was for India to be free of British rule but we also wanted the country to remain united. For a long time there had been violent racial conflict between Hindus and Muslims. The Muslims had their own organization, the Muslim League, which wanted India to be divided so that there could be an independent Muslim state. This was something that the British also supported. In 1942 I led a movement called 'Quit India', calling for immediate independence and I was arrested. In the meantime, the Muslim League promised the British

that the Indian army, whose soldiers were mainly Muslim, would continue to fight with them. This promise was on the understanding that two things would happen. Firstly, <u>negotiations</u> would begin for the British to leave India, and secondly, before they left, they would divide India to create an independent Muslim state.

In the summer of 1947, Indian independence from the British was declared. This was on the day after the British created the Muslim state of Pakistan, dividing India. My wife did not live to see the independence of India as she died in 1944. I am sure she hadn't realized what marriage to me meant – at the age of thirteen I did not know myself what I was going to do with my life. In truth, I was more married to the causes I was following than to her, but whether she knew it or not, her support kept me going. Four years later, my spirit was also set free when I was <u>assassinated</u> at a prayer meeting. <u>Ironically</u>, it was not the British or the Pakistanis that fired the gun, both of whom had their reasons for killing me, but a Hindu <u>nationalist</u>.

The Life of Mahatma Gandhi

1869   Mohandas Karamchand Gandhi was born in Porbandar, Gujarat, British India. Later in life, he was referred to as Mahatma, meaning 'great soul'.

1876   The family moved to Rajkot.

1883   At the age of 13, Gandhi married Kasturba Makhanji, in an arranged marriage.

1885   The couple's first child was born, but died a few days later.

1888   Gandhi went to England to study law at University College London. He joined the Vegetarian Society and developed an interest in religious thought.

1891   He passed the bar examination for lawyers in London. He then returned to India to discover his mother had died. He opened a law practice, which was unsuccessful.

1893   Gandhi accepted a one-year contract from an Indian firm to travel to South Africa and work as a lawyer.

1894   He helped set up the Natal Indian Congress and started to campaign for Indian rights.

1896   Gandhi returned to India and took his family back to South Africa.

1901–1902   Gandhi returned to India to attend the Indian National Congress, where he met nationalist leaders. He also opened a law firm in Mumbai.

1903   He opened a law office in Johannesburg.

1906   He led a protest against anti-Indian laws.

1907   The Transvaal Government bought in a new Act forcing registration of the Indian population.

1908   Gandhi led a mass non-violent protest using his method of *satyagraha* (devotion to the truth). Gandhi spent two months in prison.

1909   He wrote a book, *Hind Swaraj*, or *Home Rule*, as it was called in English. This was the blueprint for the Indian Independence Movement.

1913   Gandhi led 2,500 Indian miners in a protest. He was arrested and put in prison.

1914   Aged 45, he left South Africa and planned to return to India, after making a short stopover in England. While he was travelling home, the First World War broke out.

1915   Gandhi left England and returned to India. He was welcomed as a hero. He joined the Indian National Congress. As a form of protest, he began the first of many fasts.

1918–1919   Gandhi used his *satyagraha* method during the Champaran and Kheda protests. The local farmers were being forced to grow crops that they could not use themselves, but that were to be sold, and were being highly taxed. Gandhi also became a high-profile spokesperson for Muslims in the Khilafat movement.

1919   The Jallianwala Bagh massacre took place. Gandhi led the first nationwide campaign against Britain's unfair rule.

1921   Gandhi took on leadership of the India National Congress.

1922   He led a non-cooperation movement and, as a result, he was arrested and imprisoned for two years.

1925–1929   He wrote a series of articles, later called *The Story of My Experiments with Truth*.

1930   The Indian National Congress declared
        the independence of India. Gandhi led the
        385 km Dandi Salt March to protest about
        the tax on salt, and was imprisoned. He
        published the *Declaration of Independence of
        India*. The first Round Table Conference
        was held in London, where not one
        representative from the Indian National
        Congress was invited.

1931   The Gandhi–Irwin agreement was signed
        and Gandhi attended the second Round
        Table Conference in London. He also
        visited the cloth mills in the north of
        England.

1932   The Indian National Congress refused to
        attend the third Round Table Conference.
        Gandhi began a long fast to protest against
        the British Government's treatment of the
        Indian people.

1934   Gandhi launched the All India Village
        Industries Association.

1942   Gandhi led the 'Quit India' movement,
        during the Second World War. He called
        for immediate independence and was
        arrested by the British and held in Aga
        Khan Palace, Pune.

1944   His wife, Kasturba, died.

1947   The Indo–Pakistan war took place. The
        British divided the land to create Pakistan,
        and India and Pakistan were each given
        independence from British rule.

1948   Mahatma Gandhi died aged 78, as a result
        of an assassination by a Hindu nationalist,
        in New Delhi, India.

abolish TRANSITIVE VERB
If someone in authority
abolishes a practice or
organization, they put an end
to it.

apply TRANSITIVE VERB
If you **apply** a rule or piece of
knowledge, you use it in a
situation or activity.

apprentice COUNTABLE NOUN
An **apprentice** is a person who
works with someone in order to
learn their skill.

aristocracy COUNTABLE NOUN
The **aristocracy** is a class of
people in some countries who
have a high social rank and
special titles.

aristocratic ADJECTIVE
Aristocratic means belonging to
or typical of the aristocracy.

assassinate TRANSITIVE VERB
If someone important **is
assassinated**, they are murdered
as a political act.

brutal ADJECTIVE
A **brutal** act or person is cruel
and violent.

capitalism UNCOUNTABLE NOUN
Capitalism is an economic and
political system in which
property, business, and industry
are owned by private individuals
and not by the state.

cargo (cargoes) VARIABLE NOUN
The **cargo** of a ship or plane is
the goods that it is carrying.

caste COUNTABLE NOUN
A **caste** is one of the social
classes into which people in a
Hindu society are divided.

chariot COUNTABLE NOUN
In ancient times, **chariots** were
fast-moving vehicles with two
wheels that were pulled by
horses.

civil war VARIABLE NOUN
A **civil war** is a war that is fought
between different groups of
people living in the same
country.

colonist COUNTABLE NOUN
Colonists are people who start
a colony.

colony COUNTABLE NOUN
A **colony** is a country that is controlled by a more powerful country.

communism UNCOUNTABLE NOUN
Communism is the political belief that all people are equal and that workers should control the means of producing things.

communist ADJECTIVE
Communist organizations support and believe in communism.

corruption UNCOUNTABLE NOUN
Corruption is dishonesty and illegal behaviour by people in positions of power.

country estate COUNTABLE NOUN
A **country estate** is a large area of land in the country owned by one person.

cramped ADJECTIVE
A **cramped** room or building is not big enough for the people or things in it.

culture shock VARIABLE NOUN
Culture shock is a feeling of anxiety and confusion you get when you first arrive in another country because it is very different to what you are used to.

deck
below decks If someone is **below decks** on a ship, they are in the lower part of it.

dedicate TRANSITIVE VERB
If a book, song, or event **is dedicated** to someone, it is written, performed, or organized for them as a sign of affection or respect.

disobey TRANSITIVE VERB
When someone **disobeys** a person or an order, they deliberately do not do what they have been told to do.

doctorate COUNTABLE NOUN
A **doctorate** is the highest degree awarded by a university.

elder COUNTABLE NOUN
An **elder** is someone in your family or community who is older than you.

empire COUNTABLE NOUN
An **empire** is a group of countries controlled by one powerful country.

endurance UNCOUNTABLE NOUN
Endurance is the ability to continue with a difficult experience or activity over a long period of time.

ethical ADJECTIVE
If you describe something you
do as **ethical**, you mean that it
is morally right or acceptable.

ethics PLURAL NOUN
Ethics are moral beliefs and
rules about right and wrong.

famine VARIABLE NOUN
A **famine** is a serious shortage
of food in a country, which may
cause many deaths.

filth UNCOUNTABLE NOUN
Filth is a disgusting amount
of dirt.

filthy ADJECTIVE
Something that is **filthy** is very
dirty indeed.

frustration UNCOUNTABLE NOUN
Frustration is a feeling of anger
you get when you cannot do
anything about a problem.

gamble INTRANSITIVE VERB
If you **gamble**, you bet money
on the result of a game, race,
or competition.

gas TRANSITIVE VERB
To **gas** a person or animal means
to kill them by making them
breathe poisonous gas.

gather TRANSITIVE VERB,
INTRANSITIVE VERB
When people **gather**
somewhere, they come together
in a group.

greedy ADJECTIVE
Someone who is **greedy** wants
more of something than is
necessary or fair.

hardship UNCOUNTABLE NOUN
Hardship is a situation in
which your life is difficult or
unpleasant.

horrified ADJECTIVE
If someone is **horrified**, they
feel shocked, disappointed, or
disgusted.

humanities PLURAL NOUN
The **humanities** are subjects
such as literature, philosophy,
and history that are concerned
with human ideas and behaviour.

humiliating ADJECTIVE
If something is **humiliating**, it
embarrasses you and makes you
feel ashamed and stupid.

ignorance UNCOUNTABLE NOUN
Ignorance of something is lack
of knowledge about it.

immorality UNCOUNTABLE NOUN
Immorality is behaviour that is
morally wrong.

imperial ADJECTIVE
Imperial means belonging or
relating to an empire, emperor,
or empress.

inevitable ADJECTIVE
If something is **inevitable**, it is
certain to happen and cannot be
prevented or avoided.

influential ADJECTIVE
Someone who is **influential** has
a lot of influence over people or
events.

inherit TRANSITIVE VERB
If you **inherit** money, property,
or a position, you receive it from
someone who has died.

innovation COUNTABLE NOUN
An **innovation** is a new thing or
new method of doing something.
UNCOUNTABLE NOUN
Innovation is the introduction
of new things or new methods.

insecure ADJECTIVE
If you **feel insecure**, you feel
slightly worried because you
do not know what is going to
happen.

instability UNCOUNTABLE NOUN
Instability is a situation in which
something is likely to change or
come to an end suddenly.

interfere INTRANSITIVE VERB
If someone **interferes in** a
situation, they get involved in it
although it does not concern
them and their involvement is
not wanted.

interpret TRANSITIVE VERB
If you **interpret** something in a
particular way, you decide that
this is its meaning.

intolerance UNCOUNTABLE NOUN
Intolerance is unwillingness to
let other people act in a
different way or hold different
opinions from you. [DISAPPROVAL]

ironically ADVERB
You use **ironically** to draw
attention to a situation which is
odd or amusing because it
involves a contrast.

left-wing ADJECTIVE
Left-wing people, groups, or
publications have or contain
political ideas that are based
on socialism.

logic UNCOUNTABLE NOUN
Logic is the study of a way of reasoning that involves a series of statements, each of which must be true if the statement before it is true.

mass ADJECTIVE
Mass is used to describe something which involves or affects a very large number of people.

mature ADJECTIVE
If you describe someone as **mature**, you think that their behaviour is responsible and sensible.

meet (meets, meeting, met)
TRANSITIVE VERB
If something **meets** a need, requirement, or condition, it is satisfactory or sufficiently large to fulfil it.

metaphysics UNCOUNTABLE NOUN
Metaphysics is a part of philosophy which is concerned with understanding reality and developing theories about what exists and how we know that it exists.

midwife (midwives) COUNTABLE NOUN
A **midwife** is a nurse who advises pregnant women and helps them to give birth.

monopoly COUNTABLE NOUN
If a company, person, or state has a **monopoly on** something such as an industry, they have complete control over it.

motivate TRANSITIVE VERB
If someone **motivates** you **to** do something, they make you feel determined to do it.

mourn TRANSITIVE VERB,
INTRANSITIVE VERB
If you **mourn**, or **mourn** someone who has died, you are very sad that they have died and show your sorrow in the way that you behave.

mutual ADJECTIVE
You use **mutual** to describe a situation, feeling, or action that is experienced, felt, or done by both of two people mentioned.

mythology UNCOUNTABLE NOUN
Mythology is a group of myths, especially those from a particular country, religion, or culture.

nationalist COUNTABLE NOUN
A **nationalist** is a person who believes in gaining political independence for a particular group of people.

negotiate TRANSITIVE VERB, INTRANSITIVE VERB
If two people or groups **negotiate** something, they talk about a problem or an arrangement in order to solve the problem or complete the arrangement.

negotiations PLURAL NOUN
Negotiations are discussions that take place between people with different interests, in which they try to reach an agreement.

oath COUNTABLE NOUN
An **oath** is a formal promise.

obey TRANSITIVE VERB, INTRANSITIVE VERB
If you **obey** a rule, instruction, or person, you do what you are told to do.

philosophical ADJECTIVE
Philosophical means concerned with or relating to philosophy.

plantation COUNTABLE NOUN
A **plantation** is a large piece of land where crops such as cotton, tea, or sugar are grown.

possess TRANSITIVE VERB
To **possess** a quality, ability, or feature means to have it.

principle COUNTABLE NOUN
A **principle** is a belief that you have about the way you should behave.

privileged ADJECTIVE
Someone who is **privileged** has an advantage or opportunity that most other people do not have, often because of their wealth or high social class.

prosperity UNCOUNTABLE NOUN
Prosperity is a condition in which a person or community is being financially successful.

rebellion VARIABLE NOUN
A **rebellion** is a violent organized action by a large group of people who are trying to change their country's political system.

reluctant ADJECTIVE
If you are **reluctant to** do something, you do not really want to do it.

representation UNCOUNTABLE NOUN
If a group or person has **representation** in a parliament or on a committee, someone in parliament or on the committee will vote or make decisions on their behalf.

resistance UNCOUNTABLE NOUN
When there is **resistance** to an attack, people fight back.

restriction COUNTABLE NOUN
You can refer to anything that limits what you can do as a **restriction**.

rotting ADJECTIVE
Rotting food, wood, or other substances are decaying and falling apart.

sacrifice VARIABLE NOUN
A **sacrifice** is something valuable or important that you give up, usually to obtain something else.

sculptor COUNTABLE NOUN
A **sculptor** is someone who creates works of art by carving or shaping materials such as stone or clay.

slavery UNCOUNTABLE NOUN
Slavery is the system by which people are owned by other people as slaves.

spectre COUNTABLE NOUN
You talk about the **spectre** of something unpleasant when you are frightened that it might occur.

starve INTRANSITIVE VERB
If people **starve**, they suffer greatly and may die from lack of food.

stigma VARIABLE NOUN
If you say that something has a **stigma** attached to it, you mean that people consider it to be unacceptable or a disgrace, and you think this is unfair.

subservient ADJECTIVE
If you are **subservient**, you do whatever someone wants you to do.

superior ADJECTIVE
A **superior** person has more authority or importance than another person in the same organization or system.

taint TRANSITIVE VERB
If you say that something or someone **is tainted** by something undesirable or corrupt, you mean that their status or reputation is harmed by it.

theocracy VARIABLE NOUN
A **theocracy** is a society which
is ruled by priests who represent
a god.

theoretical ADJECTIVE
Theoretical means based on or
using the ideas and abstract
principles of a subject, rather
than the practical aspects of it.

tolerance UNCOUNTABLE NOUN
Tolerance is the quality of
allowing other people to say and
do as they like, even if you do not
agree or approve of it. [APPROVAL]

tribal ADJECTIVE
Tribal means relating to or
belonging to tribes.

uplift TRANSITIVE VERB
If something **uplifts** people, it
makes them happier.

will-power UNCOUNTABLE NOUN
Will-power is a very strong
determination to do something.

workhouse COUNTABLE NOUN
A **workhouse** was a place where
very poor people could live and
do unpleasant jobs in return for
food in the past.

worship TRANSITIVE VERB,
INTRANSITIVE VERB
To **worship** God means to show
your respect to God, for
example by saying prayers.

Collins English Readers

Agatha Christie

THE MURDER OF
ROGER ACKROYD

APPOINTMENT
WITH DEATH

THE MYSTERIOUS
AFFAIR AT STYLES

THE MAN IN THE
BROWN SUIT

The Queen of Crime for
English Language Learners

Twenty Agatha Christie Mysteries

CEF Level B2 • incl. CD

historical and cultural notes • character notes
glossary • online support

www.collinselt.com/agathachristie

Collins
English Readers

ALSO AVAILABLE IN THE AMAZING PEOPLE READERS SERIES:

Level 1

Amazing Leaders
978-0-00-754492-9
William the Conqueror, Saladin,
Genghis Khan, Catherine the Great,
Abraham Lincoln, Queen Victoria

Amazing Inventors
978-0-00-754494-3
Johannes Gutenberg, Louis Braille,
Alexander Graham Bell, Thomas Edison,
Guglielmo Marconi, John Logie Baird

Amazing Entrepreneurs and
Business People (May 2014)
978-0-00-754501-8
Mayer Rothschild, Cornelius Vanderbilt,
Will Kellogg, Elizabeth Arden, Walt
Disney, Soichiro Honda

Amazing Women (May 2014)
978-0-00-754493-6
Harriet Tubman, Emmeline Pankhurst,
Maria Montessori, Hellen Keller, Nancy
Wake, Eva Peron

Amazing Performers (June 2014)
978-0-00-754508-7
Glenn Miller, Perez Prado, Ella
Fitzgerald, Luciano Pavarotti, John
Lennon

Level 2

Amazing Aviators
978-0-00-754495-0
Joseph-Michel Montgolfier, Louis
Blériot, Charles Lindbergh, Amelia
Earhart, Amy Johnson

Amazing Architects and Artists
978-0-00-754496-7
Leonardo da Vinci, Christopher Wren,
Antoni Gaudí, Pablo Picasso, Frida Kahlo

Amazing Composers (May 2014)
978-0-00-754502-5
JS Bach, Wolfgang Mozart, Giuseppe
Verdi, Johann Strauss, Pyotr
Tchaikovsky, Irving Berlin

Amazing Mathematicians
(May 2014)
978-0-00-754503-2
Galileo Galilei, René Descartes, Isaac
Newton, Carl Gauss, Charles Babbage,
Ada Lovelace

Amazing Medical People
(June 2014)
978-0-00-754509-4
Edward Jenner, Florence Nightingale,
Elizabeth Garrett, Carl Jung, Jonas Salk,
Christiaan Barnard

Level 3

Amazing Explorers
978-0-00-754497-4
Marco Polo, Ibn Battuta, Christopher Columbus, James Cook, David Livingstone, Yuri Gagarin

Amazing Writers
978-0-00-754498-1
Geoffrey Chaucer, William Shakespeare, Charles Dickens, Victor Hugo, Leo Tolstoy, Rudyard Kipling

Amazing Philanthropists
(May 2014)
978-0-00-754504-9
Alfred Nobel, Andrew Carnegie, John Rockefeller, Thomas Barnardo, Henry Wellcome, Madam CJ Walker

Amazing Performers *(May 2014)*
978-0-00-754505-6
Pablo Casals, Louis Armstrong, Édith Piaf, Frank Sinatra, Maria Callas, Elvis Presley

Amazing Scientists *(June 2014)*
978-0-00-754510-0
Antoine Lavoisier, Humphry Davy, Gregor Mendel, Louis Pasteur, Charles Darwin, Francis Crick

Level 4

Amazing Scientists
978-0-00-754500-1
Alessandro Volta, Michael Faraday, Marie Curie, Albert Einstein, Alexander Fleming, Linus Pauling

Amazing Writers *(May 2014)*
978-0-00-754506-3
Voltaire, Charlotte Brontë, Mark Twain, Jacques Prevert, Ayn Rand, Aleksandr Solzhenitsyn

Amazing Leaders *(May 2014)*
978-0-00-754507-0
Julius Caesar, Queen Elizabeth I, George Washington, King Louis XVI, Winston Churchill, Che Guevara

Amazing Entrepreneurs and Business People *(June 2014)*
978-0-00-754511-7
Henry Heinz, William Lever, Michael Marks, Henry Ford, Coco Chanel, Ray Kroc

Collins
English Readers

Also available at this level

Level 4
CEF B2

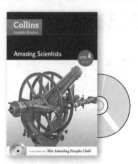

Amazing Scientists
978-0-00-754500-1

Amazing Writers
978-0-00-754506-3

Amazing Leaders
978-0-00-754507-0

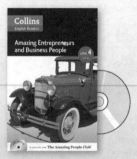

Amazing Entrepreneurs and Business People
978-0-00-754511-7

Sign up for our emails at **www.collinselt.com**
to receive free teaching and/or learning resources, as well as the most
up-to-date news about new publications, events, and competitions.

 POWERED BY COBUILD

www.collinselt.com

 @CollinsELT   /collinselt